Air Photos

Photos from the collection of Aerial Surveys Inc.

The book contains aerial photos taken of the Apulia, Fabius, LaFayette, Pompey and Tully area. These photographs are copyrighted by Aerial Surveys Inc. and are not to be reproduced without permission. Photographs of each image can be purchased by contacting:

Aerial Surveys Inc.
PO Box 12554
Rochester, NY 14612
(585) 663-8231
aerialsurveys@rochester.rr.com

ISBN-13:
978-1544237404

ISBN-10:
1544237405

compiled & published by:
J. Roy Dodge
Bill & Joanne Casey
bill5308@aol.com

3/6/2017

Air Photos

Introduction

Photographs capture a "moment in time" and are one of the tools of the historian. Postcards, in their heyday 1905-1930 have been the most common capture of these images. The series: *Images of America* have published a number of books showing photos and postcards concentrating on a neighborhood or town.

As photography techniques improved and the cameras became more portable, partially due to the efforts to utilized air photography in World War 1, cities began to hire photographers to capture images for planning purposes. The City of Syracuse hired **Airmap Corporation of America** in 1926 to photograph and create photo maps of the city. These maps were considered indispensable by the city staff. These 1926 photographs are held by the Onondaga Historical Association.

During the FDR administration, many make work projects were created. Once such project was to photograph the total land mass of the USA. As this was a very large project, it had to completed over a number of years. In New York State, most of the work was completed by CS Robinson from Ithaca, NY. The earliest photos were taken from 1936 thru 1938. They can be viewed online: http://aerial-ny.library.cornell.edu/browse/. This collection also includes photos as late as 1991.The FDR administration collection only has a straight down view showing building roofs and outlines of farm fields. It is not very useful in investigating architecture of the many buildings.

Starting in the 1940's photographers started taking air photographs on speculation, with the hopes to sell the images to home and farm owners. The earliest in New York State were Henry Mason between 1946 and 1953 and Henry DeWolf 1940's thru 1980's. Nothing remains of the Mason collection so should you have a photo, cherish it as it can't be reprinted. Henry DeWolf's photographic works has been maintained and is still available to purchase.

Purpose

The purpose of this publication is to encourage the reader to discover the "moment in time" that these photographs have captured. With the changing agricultural technology, few of these "once was" farms still exists today. In the event that a photo is special, perhaps grandpas farm from a previous generation, this book allows a second opportunity for the viewer to consider buying a print.

J. Roy Dodge and Bill Casey have been able to view some of the negatives after discovering which film rolls are in the area of interest: Apulia, LaFayette, Fabius, LaFayette, and Tully. We have made digital copies of some of these negatives and/or photos and have elected to share them with the printing of this book. The images in this publication in no way includes all the photos of the area but merely is what we have been able to identify and obtain to date. We want to thank everyone that have helped us photograph their images and use their images to guide us into this vast collection.

The quality of the images in this publication is not a reflection on the fine quality of the negatives held in the collection. In an effort to make a book of reasonable price we have chosen to print in medium quality and in black & white to control the cost to the buyer. Any photographic print will be many times higher in quality and can be printed in many sizes and cropped as the buyer wishes.

Dates of the Images

Roll 22 1953, Roll 23 1953, Roll 227 9/7/1957, Roll 242 4/2/1958, Roll 245 4/9/1958
Roll C3 Oct 1963, Roll C9 5/12/1964

All images in the book can be purchased from Aerial Surveys:

Aerial Surveys (585) 663-8231

PO Box 125554

Rochester, NY 14612

email: aerialsurveys@rochester.rr.com

22-104 Palmer Feed Mill

22-107 Hills Gas Station along Route 20

22-112 Andrew Shanahan farm corner of Route 20 & Berry Road

22-113 Frank Carroll Farm Route 20

22-116 Edward Carroll farm along Route 20

22-156 Jerome farm just west of Route 91 S curves, Fabius, NY Owned by Duanne Skeele. Barn lost top fire.

23-103 Big Bend Gas Station corner of Route 20 and Jamesville Apulia Road

23-105 House and saw mill corner of Palmer and Clark Hollow Roads

23-111 Charles Adsit farm on Eager Road

23-112 Sam Share farm #2 on Eager Road

23-113 Victor Sessler farm on Eager Road

23-114 Ernest Bishop & Donald Deenan farm on Eager Road

23-116 Fred Eager farm on Coye Road

23-145 Slosson farm on Sweet Road, Pompey, NY

227-105 Tully Central School note the track

227-106 Tully Bowling Pin Factory, note the large piles of sawdust

227-107 Spot
Oil Company

227-108 Tully Bldg
and Tully GLF

227-109 Tully GLF

227-110 View looking northwest of the center of the Tully Village

227-111 Tully Village looking west

227-112 View of Tully Village looking north

227-113

227-114 Ousby's "tenant farm" on Tully Truxton Road

227-1145 Ousby residence and farm Tully Truxton Road

227-116 2nd view of the Ousby farm and residence

227-117 Regan farm lower side of Route 80, June farm just above

227-118 Donald and Gerald June farm

227-119 Ernest Bishop farm later owned by the Baker family, corner of Route 80 and Markham Hollow Road

227-120 Otie Smith farm and home. Barns are built in the Louck style and were used in their advertisements. Farm later purchased by the Luchsinger family.

227-121 Hughes farm and home.
Later became Hill & Dale Golf Course

227-122 Sales Barn and Mitchell
Cabbage houses in Apulia Station

227-123 View of Apulia Station South Street, Chair Factory and Milk Plant

227-124 Farm and home of the Olcott family, was earlier owned by Stephen Shea and then Duane Hunsinger

227-125 View of Apulia Station from the east. Case farm (now Maple Lane Manor) to the right, Neal Mowery farm to the left. Mitchell cabbage houses middle left.

227-127 Cooper Dairy on Route 91 Apulia, NY, Porter cows to the right

227-128 Farm and home of Leland Houck along Route 91

227-129 Farm and home of John Parman on Jones Road just off Route 91. Later purchased by Elm Crest Girls Center

227-130 View of the hamlet of Apulia from the south. AB Porter farm in center

22-131 Donald Casey farm and home along Route 80 in Apulia. Gorman farm upper left.

227-132 Gorman farm and home. Later purchased by Agway Inc

227-133 Randall farm and home at St John's Corner intersection of Berwyn and Route 80. House and barns removed for Agway headquarters.

227-134 Herlihy farm and home on Herlihy Road later purchased by Bill Risser and then Agway

227-135 William Tallon farm and home at St. John's Corner Berwyn and Route 80. Later purchased by Agway.

227-136 Hartnett farm and home, later purchased by Casey Bros. now the location of Neil D. Casey Farm Market.

227-137 Lee and Annie Fish farm and home at the end of Matson Road. The Fish family started farming here in 1939.

227-138 Donald Casey farm
looking to the west

227-139 Hamlet of Apulia
looking to the west

227-140 Al Hill's gas station and repairs shop with parts stored behind, Nellie Casey's house and chicken coops, now owned by Dean Wadsworth

227-141 Kogut's house and chicken business and old Apulia School house, Bookhounds house and barn just below.

227-142 Farm owned by John Casey, home of Bill & Joanne Casey Berry Road, Apulia, NY

227-143 Hamlet of Apulia Station, NY looking to the west showing Mitchell's Cabbage Houses, Apulia Hotel

227-144 Ceylon Case farm and home, later purchase by Hunsinger and now owned by Maple Lane Manor

227-145 Green farm and home at the end of South Street in Apulia Station

227-146 Hamlet of Apulia Station showing the coal trestle, train depot, Apulia Hotel, Briggs Store

227-147 The Blaney family farms later purchased by Frank Blaney and operated as a single farm

227-148 Intersection of Jamesville Apulia , Garrett and Daley Roads. Cows on the right are Elmor Craw's, cows to the left are the Garrett's

227-149 Arlington Garrett farm and home along the Jamesville Apulia Road

227-150 Home of Ruth Smith

227-151 Farm and home of Robert Tompkins, note hay still being stacked in piles.

227-152 Farm at June's Crossing Jamesville Apulia Road and DL&W Railroad. Farm owned by Wolcott, then Fairchild/Jenks. Barn built 1903.

227-126 AB Porter farm and home corner of Route 80 and Route 91.

227-153 Van Smith farm, formerly, Jay Brown and son Howard. Formerly E. Clark property.

227-154 Hart's Rendering & B&B Body Shop

227-155 Parks farm now owned by the Doupe family

227-156 Property owned by Mrs. Sherameda, house and barns now gone.

227-157 Joseph Bocak farm and home, formerly owned by Leonard

227-158 Fox farm and home also known as the Everingham farm

227-159 Nurse farm once owned by the Everinghams

227-160 Hart's Rendering and B&B Body Shop

227-161 Paul Morezak residence. Childhood home of Helen Morezak Bobbett

227-162 Farm and home of Van Smith. Was the farm of Jay and son Howard Brown.

227-163 Jenk's (Fairchild) farm and home at June's Crossing

227-164 Sky High Farm on SkyHigh Road. Once owned and operated by Syracuse University

227-165 Tweeze Preston farm and home on Sky High Road

227-166 Ken Winslow farm and home

227-176 Aldrich farm on SkyHigh Road

227-168 Hockrighter farm and home corner of SkyHigh and Route 80.

227-169 Ellis farm and home Rout 80
227-170 Ellis farm and home Route 80

245-13 Solvay Farm on
Route 11A
245-14 Solvay Farm
Route 11A

245-15

245-16 Henderson farm Route 11A

245-18 Shue Farm

245-19 Howard Sipfle farm

245-22

245-23 Paul Burt Farm
Route 11A

245-25 View of hamlet of Cardiff looking north. Route 20 runs right to left. Route 11A runs from lower right to upper left .

Oct 1963 Henry DeWolf's flight records note that he has started using color film. The following photos are all taken in color but we have elected to print this book in black and white. Please note that all photos now have a "C" before the film roll number eg. C3-214.

C3-214 Harold Dodge farm on the Jamesville Apulia Road

C3-215 Bush Farm aloneg the Jamesville Apulia Road

C3-236 Henson Farm
Equipment Route 11
LaFayette, NY

C3-237

C3-236

C3-333 Hill & Dale Farm along Rowley Jerome Road, Fabius, NY

C3-441 Hamlet of LaFayette, NY
view toward the west

C8-437 Farm owned by Otis Young along Route 13, Truxton, NY. Now the location of Trinity Dairy

C9-41 Octagon School house Route 11A

C9-47 Farm overlooking Interstate 81

C9-50
C9-233 LaFayette Hamlet

C9-327 House along S curves Route 91

C9-328 Home of Ed Skeele S curves Route 91 Pompey,NY

C9-331 Marky Glasgow farm, his home is north of the photo

C9-332 Rowley farm part of the Hill & Dale Farm Rowley Jerome Road

C9-341 Photo shows the farm of Gene Terrill on the west side of the Village of Fabius, NY. Duba's chicken barn is at the top of the photo. The chicken coop was once the home of the Fabius Creamery.

C9-342

Fabius Central School along Main Street Route 80 View is from the north

C-9 451

Farm and home owned by Otie Smith later purchased by the Luchsinger family. Located along Route 80 Apulia, NY

C9-452

Hughes farm is just being converted to Hill & Dale Golf Course Route 80 Tully, NY

C9-453

The home of Greta Case in the hamlet of Apulia Station, NY

C9-454 Lower right is the office of the Morezak Brothers heating business. Lower center is the train depot no longer used by the railroad but used by the Morezak Brothers. Center of the photo is the Apulia Auction barns. The Auction barns had been Mitchell's cabbage storage. Building beyond to the left is the old Borden/Dairylea Creamery owned by the Woodford Bros. Construction. Upper fields are the back of the Hughes farm now converted to Hill & Dale Gold Course. Photo is taken from the north side of Route 80 in Apulia Station, NY

C9-455

Green Hilfinger farm and home on South Street Apulia Station, NY.

Hill & Dale Gold Course along the railroad tracks in upper portion of photo.

C9-456

The home to the Gorman family once they sold their farm to Agway Inc. Located along Route 80 Apulia Station, NY

C9-457

Farm and home of Stephen Shea brother of Mike Shea, later sold to the Olcutt family. Now the farm is owned by Maple Lane Manor farm.

C9-458

View of the western side of the hamlet of Apulia, NY along Route 80. Henderson home and barn lower center. Old Pea Vinery to the left. Cooper Dairy at the top of photo.

C9-459 The home of Marlin and Bob Brown along Route 91 just of Route 80 in Apulia, NY

C9-460 Home of the Rutherford family Route 91

C9-461 House just south of Rutherford. Leland Houck's farm field just behind homes.

C9-462 Tenant house on Labrador Farm, later the home of Leland Houck once he sold the farm to Agway Inc.

C9-463 Labrador Farm home to the Leland Houck family. Photo taken viewing the hamlet of Apulia to the north

C9-464

Farm owned by John Parmon later sold to ElmCrest Girls Center. Farm is located on the the deadend Jones Road just off Route 91

C9-465

The home of the Fairchild family along Route 91.

C9-466 The home of the Holcomb family Route 91

C9-467 Farm & home of AB Porter family

C9-468

Lower portion of photo is the home and farm of Donald Casey. Farm and home in center of the photo is Tim, Tom, and Mary Hartnett. Farm right is the barn of the Tallon farm located on St. John's Corner Route 80 and Berwyn Road

C9-469

Al Hill's Gas Station and Repair Shop. Auto parts storage (junk yard) behind. Tallon home to the left, once they sold their farm to Agway Inc.

C9-470

Farm owned by John Casey Berry Road and Daley Road. House and farm now owned by Bill & Joanne Casey

C9-472

The Case family farm. Roscoe (father) transferred to son Ceylon. Barns burned in later years when owned by Hunsinger. Now owned by Maple Lane Manor farms.

C9-473

Elmer Craw farm and home. Elmer milked and bottled his own milk. House in lower portion of photo is Cliff Adams

C9-474

The home and farm of Ed and Doris Luchsinger Lucky Lane Farm on Lucky Lane Road just off Daley Road. Home to Jersey cows.

C9-475

Home and outbuildings of Cliff Adams on the Daley Road

C9-476

House and barns along Jamesville Apulia Road and Daley Road

C9-477

Farm and home of Arlington Garrett along the Jamesville Apulia Road. View from the north.

C9-478

Home of Ruth Smith sister of Frank Blaney along the Jamesville Apulia Road.

C9-479

Farm and home at June's Crossing at the Jamesville Apulia Road and railroad. Barn built in 1903. Farm previously owned by Jencks and Farichilds.

C9-480

Farm and home of Robert Tompkins. New barn built in 1930's after the previous barn burned.

C9-481

Arlington Garrett farm and home along the Jamesville Apulia Road.

C9-482

Farms and home of Frank Blaney. Farms once operated by separate Blaney families. Photo taken along the Jamesville Apulia Road

C9-483

The home and apple orchard of the Kelly family in Apulia Station, NY.

House was once the Apulia Station school. Note the fire house was not built yet.

C9-486

Home and farm owned by the Ellis family. Barns lost to fire. Land still owned and worked by the Ellis family.

C9-489

Farm and home of Ken Winslow on Skyhigh Road Tully, NY

C10-500

Keenview Farm in Cuyler, NY owned by Barbra and Richard Keeney

C253-113

John Casey Farm, home of Bill & Joanne Casey. Corner of Daley & Berry Roads

C253-122

Hill & Dale Farm and home of Duanne & Edna Skeele. Along Rowley Jerome Road Fabius, NY

C253-144

Hill & Dale Farm Upper house residence of Duanne & Edna, lower house Harvey Skeele

C253-167 DeRuyter Lake view from the south looking north

C937-88 Hill & Dale Farm Rowley Jerome Road, Fabius, NY looking northwest. Freestall and machinery shop additions.